THE FAST AND EASY GUIDE TO POWERFUL AUTHOR BRANDING

RACHEL THOMPSON

Copyright © 2022 by Rachel Thompson

All rights reserved. This book or parts thereof may not be reproduced in any form, stored in any retrieval system, or transmitted in any form by any means— electronic, mechanical, photocopy, recording, or otherwise—without prior written permission of the publisher, except as provided by United States of America copyright law.

AUTHOR BRANDING

Whether your books are available yet or not, figuring out your personal (author) branding is the foundation for everything you'll do regarding your posts, visuals, pods, Spaces (social audio), social media, blogging, articles, quotes, newsletter…everything.

Think of your author platform as a *deck*. Each tactic mentioned above is a *plank*. You can add each plank and hope for results, or strategically lay your branding *foundation* down first to hold all the planks firmly.

Let's start by defining branding. We'll review several critical aspects of discovering your author branding and provide further reading.

What Does Personal (Author) Branding Mean?

Branding is the intersection of your interests, sharing experiences, and connecting with readers. It's a strategic exercise that will affect all your book marketing tactics.

Research shows that shoppers are 55% more likely to buy products from brands with a story they like, 44% will share the story, and 15% will buy the product immediately.

Think Ikigai! (ee-key-guy)

Say what? Yes, ikigai is a beautiful Japanese concept to help people find meaning in their lives. Let's find your ikigai:

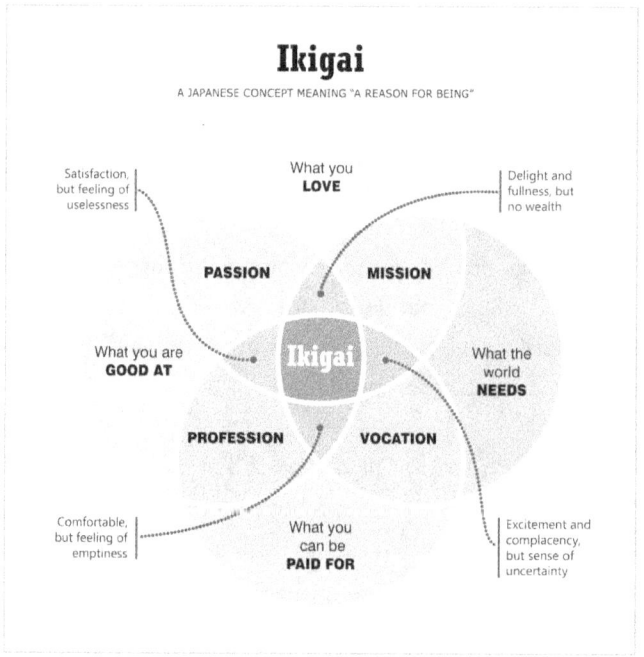

What is *Your* Branding?

Branding stumps many writers. I had to figure it out for both my author and business accounts. Each has completely different branding, given that one version is for memoir and poetry while the other is for my business. For most writers, one social author account on the leading platforms (e.g., Twitter, Facebook, Instagram, etc.) will do the job; I mean you, the writer, in all the places readers can find you.

As writers, we know all about storytelling, and that's what your branding is — sharing stories, data, quotes, etc., about the topics you're most interested in, are an expert on, or want to learn more about.

Think like a reader.

- How do you find good books?
- What do you want to know about the writers you love?
- Beyond their writing motivation, what is their goal in writing the book?
- How do they spend their days?
- Do they cook, have pets, and love Real Housewives?

You are more than your writing. You are a three-dimensional human with thoughts, experiences, and emotions. Sharing these types of posts will make you relatable, and as shown above, people buy from people they relate to. Share the joy *and* the challenges.

Branding connects you to your reader. What's your authentic self? That's what we want to share.

What's your awesome? Let's share it!

Does Genre Matter?

Nope. Regardless of the genre or multiple genres you write in, marketing is marketing and branding,.

You still need social media to connect with readers, bloggers, agents, and publishers (if you choose to go that route). You still need fresh content on your site, optimized blog posts to be more visible, and Google to scrape your site. Options include interviews, providing value (e.g., sharing content by you or others on your topics of interest), and building relationships.

Are There Particular Steps or Processes Involved?

Yes, however, you don't need a degree in marketing to do this. Here is an easy, four-step process to help you:

1. **Define your message** *(e.g., I write books so other trauma survivors feel less alone)*
2. **Understand your target audience** *(e.g., most people who experience sexual trauma before the age of 18 are women, ergo, that's my target audience)*
3. **Build your narrative** *(e.g., what do I want other survivors to know about living with the aftermath of sexual abuse?)*
4. **Compose your story** *(e.g., here are my thoughts and experiences)*

(Model Source: WixBlog)

This is a helpful exercise to continually ask yourself about marketing activities, including your writing and blogging.

We Need Examples!

Great, let's do it.

When I decided to re-brand my author account, I knew what I wanted and didn't like. My first two books are satirical humor about relationships. While they did well, I knew that my next release, *Broken Pieces*, would have to have completely different branding because it's about a serious subject: surviving childhood sexual abuse and how that affected me as a woman, mother, and partner.

Since **we brand the author, not only the book**, I had some work to do.

What did that look like in practicality? I first identified the keywords and key phrases that helped define not only what I wrote about in *Pieces* but also the topics surrounding it to create my author branding:

- relationships
- sexuality
- psychology/mental health
- emotions
- memoir/narrative nonfiction

I also have some 'back-up' keywords, which are light and fun:

- cats
- lack of cooking skills
- books I love
- music
- shows
- trash tv (*Love Is Blind*, anyone?)

This is my branding **foundation**, as described above. When I post something, I look to my keywords/phrases* and type those into places to find content, e.g., social media, blogs, posts, quotes (mine and others), video, audio, etc., and schedule (using Hootsuite or Buffer — both have free options), or post live in the moment.

Your branding also encompasses your social media banners — what's your color story (e.g., which colors will you use consistently across your entire platform)?

*My business account is separate and so are those branding keywords. Having only one set of keywords would make no sense as the goals for both my author and business accounts are different.

What is Your Author Branding Foundation?

Write down the answers to these questions, which cover your strengths, passions, and interests:

- What are you most interested in?

- What do you have expert knowledge about?

- What do you love learning about?

- What do you wish more people knew?

- What do you want to learn more about?

- What do you advocate for?

- What do you enjoy?

I suggest no more than five to seven main topics as your keywords and phrases to, plus five or so backup topics.

This does not mean your author branding is set in stone. As I matured in writing, I rebranded to fit my new direction. *Branding is about setting expectations with your readers and creating connections.*

Common Questions:

Q: *Do I need new accounts for every new book?*
A: No, not at all. Having multiple book accounts can confuse and fatigue your readers because they become used to certain information from you. However, I suggest signing up for a social media management tool to help you manage your content (e.g., Hootsuite, Buffer, Later, etc.).

You are you are you — that's your branding ~ Christine Gritmon, Branding Expert.

Q: *Is branding about my media?*
A: That and so much more. Branding is everything you share: *blog posts, social media posts, articles, quotes, videos, audio, everything.*

So, not just your colors or fonts. It's also your interests and connection points.

(It does help to set up a *style guide* which gives people you work with, e.g., graphic designer, your colors, fonts, etc., so everything is, again, consistent. This is not required, but it's very helpful.)

I also recommend creating a *media kit* with a short bio and long bio, an author photo, links to your social media, publication info, or other pertinent links. You can see mine here.

Q: *Do I need to hire someone to help me? I'm lost.*
A: Your call. Many people hire me to help them determine their keywords and key phrases and learn how to optimize these efforts (aka, make it work!). Clients might work with me anywhere from three to six months to years.

I now also have affordable audit and recommendation packages available. Take a look!

Q: *How does experiencing trauma and having that as a keyword create a brand? And won't I cheapen the experience by sharing it?*

A: Again, your call. I had these same fears. Trauma is a formidable share; however, we have every right to tell our stories. We did nothing wrong. And remember: Nobody will see your writing until you decide.

```
You own everthing that
happened to you.

Tell your stories.

If people wanted you to
write warmly about them,
they should have behaved
better.

-Anne Lamott
```

Boom.

Now you have some essential tools to help you discover your author branding. Do the exercises above, and please let me know how it goes.

FURTHER READING

• *Why Branding Confuses You and How to Fix That Right Now* https://buff.ly/2LKKGGw by *@BadRedheadMedia*

You may 'just want to write,' but I challenge that notion. Writing is excellent, which is why we're authors, **but don't you want people to read what you've written?** Don't you want to make people think? Feel an emotion? Incite them to act?

• *How To Brand Yourself as A Writer — Wait! No! as an "Author"* https://buff.ly/3LorMBq by *@ChuckWendig*

• *Personal Branding for Authors: What It Is and Why It's Essential* https://buff.ly/36Httv1 by *@writerplatform*. Terrific series by Kimberly Grabas

• *4 Steps That Drive Success with Personal Branding via @TwitterBusiness* https://buff.ly/3tm20Hz

CONCLUSION

Have more questions? Purchase my *30-Day Book Marketing Challenge* now! And don't forget to attend my free weekly @BadRedheadMedia #BookMarketingChat on @TwitterSpaces every Wednesday at 11 am PST/2 pm EST. Spaces are audio-only.

Join my #BookMarketingChat Twitter community as well.

Talk soon!

I appreciate your purchase and would love it if you'd take a few minutes to *review this book* on Amazon, Goodreads, BookBub (and other sites if you have the time). Readers decide to purchase a book based on word of mouth, and your opinion counts.

ABOUT THE AUTHOR

Rachel Thompson released the ***BadRedhead Media 30-Day Book Marketing Challenge*** in December 2016 to rave reviews. She is constantly updating the book, and released a newly updated version in 2020 in both ebook and print.

She is the author of the award-winning, best-selling ***Broken Places* (one of IndieReader's "Best of 2015"** top books and 2015 Honorable Mention Winner in both the Los Angeles and the San Francisco Book Festivals), and the bestselling, multi-award-winning ***Broken Pieces*** (as well as two additional humor books, *A Walk In The Snark* and *Mancode: Exposed)*.

Broken People was released in late 2022, and won 'Best in Category' for Nonfiction with the Book Excellence Awards. Read **here** for more info!

Rachel's work is also featured in ***Feminine Collective*** anthologies (see **Books** for details).

She owns **BadRedhead Media**, creating effective social media and book marketing campaigns for authors. Her articles appear regularly in ***The Huffington Post***, ***Feminine Collective***, ***Indie Reader*** **Medium**, **OnMogul**, **Blue Ink Review**, and several others.

Not just an **advocate** for sexual abuse survivors, Rachel is the creator and founder of the hashtag phenomenon **#MondayBlogs** and the live weekly Twitter chats, **#SexAbuseChat**, co-hosted with **Cee Streetlights** and **Judith Staff** (Tuesdays, 6 pm PST/9 pm EST), and **#BookMarketingChat**, co-hosted with Melissa Flickinger and Dr. Alexandria Szeman (Wednesdays, 6 pm PST/9 pm EST).

She hates walks in the rain, running out of coffee, and coconut. A single mom, she lives in California with her two kids and two cats, where she daydreams of Thor and vaguely remembers what sleep is.

For contact information, visit rachelintheoc.com or **BadRedhead Media** at badredheadmedia.com.

ALSO BY RACHEL THOMPSON

The BadRedhead Media 30-Day Book Marketing Challenge

- 2017 Readers' Favorite Silver Award Winner (Non-Fiction)!
- 5/5 STARS, Readers Favorite!
- 4/4 STARS, IndieReader! THE SINGLE BEST TOOL every writer needs NOW to build, boost, and grow their author platform.

THE SINGLE BEST TOOL every writer needs NOW to build, boost, and grow their author platform. Unsure how to market your book or feel overwhelmed by the sheer number of author platform options out there (or not even sure what the term means)?

Ever wish someone could break it down for you in simple steps?

Then this is the book for you!

Over the course of one month, Rachel provides you daily challenges containing a wealth of information, and easy-to-follow assignments to help energize your book sales. If you haven't released your book yet, this book will help you set the stage necessary to build the strongest foundation possible for success.

Topics include:

- Twitter secrets
- Facebook page must-do's
- Social media ideas you might not know or haven't thought of
- Promotion, giveaways, and other book marketing secrets
- Website, blogging, and SEO tips designed just for authors

All writers, bloggers, and small businesses can benefit from this guide.

https://geni.us/30DayMarketing

Available in e-book and paperback

BadRedhead Media: How to Best Optimize Blog Posts for SEO: 25 Tested Tips Writers Need to Know Now

Are you unsure how to generate more traffic to your blog? *Then this is the book for you!*

Are you overwhelmed by all the SEO articles (or not even sure what the term means)? Do you wish someone could break it down for you in simple steps?

Rachel provides you with her **Top 25 Tips** in easy-to-understand language gleaned from her own ten years of successful blogging and optimizing and managing countless client blogs. Containing a wealth of information, these tips will help you increase traffic to your site!

Topics include:

- SEO terms defined
- Specific ways to increase traffic to your blog right now
- How to optimize each post for maximum exposure on Google
- Ways to connect with readers
- How to integrate your blog posts on the various social media sites

If SEO confuses you, this is an excellent beginner breakdown for any new blogger, writer, veteran author, and even small business.

Buy your copy NOW and start increasing your visibility!

Available in kindle from: http://geni.us/SEOBlogPosts

Broken Places A Memoir of Abuse

2016 Bronze Winner Readers' Favorite (NonFiction)

5/5 Stars Readers' Favorite Review Winner

2015 Best of Books, IndieReader (NonFiction)

2015 Honorable Mention Winner Los Angeles Book Festival

2015 Honorable Mention Winner San Francisco Book Festival

Award-winning author Rachel Thompson courageously confronts the topics of sexual abuse and suicide, love, and healing in her second nonfiction book of prose: *Broken*

Places. The sequel to Rachel's first award-winning, best-selling nonfiction book, *Broken Pieces*, Rachel bares her soul in essays, poems, and prose, honestly addressing life's most difficult topics. As you follow one woman's journey through the

dark and into the light, you will find yourself forever changed.

Rachel's first book in this series, *Broken Pieces*, has been a #1 best seller on Amazon (eBooks) on Women's Poetry and Abuse. Please note that this book discusses serious topics and is only intended for mature audiences.

One of IndieReader's "Best of 2015" top books and 2015 Honorable Mention Winner in both the Los Angeles and the San Francisco Book Festivals and several other awards, Broken Places, will capture your mind, body, and soul.

Kindle: http://geni.us/BrokenPlacesE

Paperback: http://geni.us/BrokenPlacesP

Broken Pieces (Essays Inspired By Life)

5/5 Stars Readers' Favorite Review Winner

2013 eFestival of Words Best Non-Fiction (General) Winner

2014 Kindle Book Award Non-Fiction Finalist

2013 eBook Cover Design Award Gold Star Winner

2013 San Francisco Book Festival Honorable Mention

2013 Global eBook Award Women Studies Non-Fiction Gold Medal Winner

Not easy subjects -- childhood sexual abuse, love, loss, date rape, grief -- but real ones, told in pieces (thus the title). *Broken Pieces* is a work of non-fiction.

Poetry, prose, and essays to let you into one woman's life -- a searingly raw examination of topics most people avoid.

Already an international #1 best seller on Amazon (eBooks) on Women's Poetry and Abuse, this book is recommended for mature audiences only due to adult themes. For more of Rachel's work, look at Rachel's second award-winning book, Broken Places, which continues the story.

Available from:

Kindle: http://geni.us/BrokenPiecesE

Paperback: http://geni.us/BrokenPiecesP

Broken People

(winner, biography, Book Excellence Awards) https://geni.us/BrokenPeople

Long before the #MeToo movement, Rachel Thompson started sharing what it was like to grow up and live with the constant trauma of childhood sexual abuse, sexual harassment, and other sexual crimes in her award-winning memoirs, Broken Pieces and Broken Places.

Broken People is the third book in this series, where she continues to explore, through hard-hitting essays and lyrical poetry, the difficulties and joys of navigating relationships, healing, and love in an environment not always conducive to survivors.

If you're a survivor or know one, you need this book.

Available from: https://geni.us/BrokenPeople

SNEAK PEEK FOR HOW TO BEST OPTIMIZE BLOG POSTS FOR SEO: 25 TESTED TIPS WRITERS NEED TO KNOW NOW

When I talk with authors about <u>optimizing their blog posts for SEO</u> (Search Engine Optimization), most look at me as though I'm speaking in tongues. And maybe I am: SEO *is* a different language when you think about it. Authors aren't socialized to learn this stuff. It's only through understanding the importance of book marketing, and <u>how SEO fits</u> into our author platform, that we realize, "holy moly, this optimization stuff truly does have an impact — maybe I should take it more seriously," and so we do.

Well, some of us anyway.

What is Blog Optimization?

According to <u>Hubspot</u>:

> *When you optimize your web pages — including your blog posts — you're making your website more visible to people who are looking for keywords associated with your brand, product, or service via search engines like Google.*

Once I got serious about this publishing career thingy, I studied, took classes, hired a professional (Barb Drozdowich of **Bakerview Consulting,** who is amazing) and switched to WordPress.org (from Blogger — if you're an author, self-hosted WordPress (aka WordPress.org) is, by far, the preferred publishing platform of the industry). My decades in Big Pharma didn't prepare me for the enormity of the multitude of tasks required for online publishing, but it certainly helped me to embrace it.

And now I want to help you do the same.

Pick up your copy today: http://geni.us/SEOBlogPosts

SNEAK PEEK FOR THE BADREDHEAD MEDIA 30-DAY BOOK MARKETING CHALLENGE

Introduction

Hello, Challenge Takers! Rachel here (aka *BadRedhead Media*). So proud of you for taking on this challenge -- you can do this! Book marketing (or blog or business) can be overwhelming. I know -- I've done all three, and still do all three every single day. I feel you.

Who is BadRedhead Media?
Here's my deal: After 17+ years in soul-sucking Big Pharma (sales, marketing, and training, now recovered, thank you), I started my blog, RachelintheOC back wow, in '08. Mostly because like you, I had something to say. I embraced blogging and social media like a dog to a bone. Blogger, Facebook, Twitter — yea! Okay…I'm here everyone. Now what? *crickets*

Perhaps many of you feel the same. And *that's* where I come in. Utilizing my almost two decades of sales, marketing, and training, plus my own experiences in social media and publishing, I learned how to brand myself, what pre-release activities work prior to book launch, all about Amazon, and what it takes to make my four books (***Broken Places,***

Broken Pieces, *A Walk In The Snark, and The Mancode: Exposed*) Number One bestsellers.

I own BadRedhead Media, creating effective social media and book marketing campaigns for authors. My articles appear regularly in *The Huffington Post*, *Feminine Collective*, *Indie Reader*, *OnMogul*, *Transformation Is Real*, *Blue Ink Review*, *Book Machine*, and several others.

I started this challenge to give you the best tips I've learned over my ten+ years in blogging and publishing, and to help you take advantage of what I've learned since I started my professional career in sales and marketing back in 1987. *Much* has changed, of course, but I learned so much about how to treat people, what works, and what doesn't. I apply those principles daily connecting with readers, bloggers, reviewers, influencers, and to continue to establish not only my brand as an author, but also as a businessperson with my own clients. Learn all about me here: BadRedheadMedia.com

It's important to note that if you are marketing a book, this challenge takes into account that your book is well-written, professionally edited, formatted, and designed. This challenge will *not* address the writing aspects of your book, except to say that a poorly written book packaged and marketed beautifully is still a poorly written book. Readers are discriminating and will crucify you in reviews. If your writing is not at the level it needs to be, take your time to make it exceptional.

If you haven't published yet, this challenge is perfect for setting up your author platform and pre-marketing your work. If you aren't an author and have no plans to be, cool. Take these tips for your blogging platform or small business.

Each day, I will assign you one tip (minimum), as well as the reasoning behind it, examples, visuals, the how-to, and the links. Do as much or as little as you want. Some will be more challenging for you, some brain-dead easy. My goal is to help as many people as possible in various stages of experience. If you still are confused after an assignment, Google for more info, go to the sites I mention directly, click on the many, *many* links I provide, or try YouTube for tutorials. The truth is out there.

Let's do this thingy.

Pick up your copy today! https://geni.us/30DayMarketing

www.ingramcontent.com/pod-product-compliance
Lightning Source LLC
Chambersburg PA
CBHW070740020526
44118CB00035B/1776